Triage

poems by

Angela LeBlanc

Finishing Line Press
Georgetown, Kentucky

Triage

ACKNOWLEDGMENTS

The author would like to thank Pete LeBlanc, Kathryn Bayne, and David Blair.

Publisher: Leah Maines
Editor: Christen Kincaid
Cover Art and Design: Kaitlyn Crowley
Author Photo: Vyanka Marinez

Table of Contents

Special Thanks
to
My husband who held my hand in the darkness.
My family who nurtured and supported me throughout.
David Blair, mentor and guide. Sylvia Plath's tulips.
Friends who lifted me up
and the readers who listened.

Narrative Arc and Sequence

The narrative arc and sequence of the pieces I have gathered for this collection is one of triage. Triage is the healing process experienced normally within a hospital confine. This perspective of the hospital experience is used by many poets labeled Neurotic or Confessionalist. This collection will create the effect of traveling through lost memories and experiences that have crippled my psyche and will examine the tender process of healing I have had to experience in order to finally be whole. This collection of poetry speaks of my past brokenness, multiple places of trauma, and the outcome of my own mental health.

Although I never found myself in a hospital room, like Anne Sexton or Sylvia Plath, interrupted from the torment of life and living—medicated and sterile, I have painfully dragged myself across years of wasteland, living my life broken and sick. I lived in constant seeking of approval: co-dependently searching to be enough. I became a chameleon, changing and morphing into whatever was needed. Multiple nights I pondered my own escape—perhaps death, solitude, failure; instead, I always held it together hoping someone would notice that I mattered. Hoping I was needed. This poetry shows that journey and the realization that I found through this writing that I had created a false hope. I had lost my identity in order to be protected from a horrific past of which I had no memory of: fragments of trauma that seep through a foggy reminiscence. It shows the healing that I have found through writing and introspection. Indeed triage.

Author's Preface

Writing is an activity that allows my spirit to come alive. For years I suffered from crippling anxiety and felt trapped under blankets of fog. This fog created a buffer, allowing me to move through life in a normal setting, one of naivety and ignorance to the trauma that surrounded me. I grew up in a very spiritual environment and was terrified of demonic activity. I remember my mother anointing the doorways each night, praying for our safety from my crazed and drunken father. She protected me the only way she knew how: with religion. That faith and hope I had in God did indeed protect me, but it created this force that crippled my understanding of reality.

As a child, I hid the terrors of my own reality behind a mask of perfection and a sweet smile. I thought that if everyone loved me, or the idea of me, no one would ever ask about my home or my family life. As I grew older, I found myself isolated and separated from my peers. This is where I tried to find solace in my talents: writing and artwork. My journals were filled with stories, poetry, rants, and tears. I read anything I could get my hands on. I once read a poem I had written aloud to my classmates in 10th grade and was mortified by the response I was given. Fellow students sneered and made remarks, making fun of the person they thought I was, making jokes that they didn't even knew I spoke. This did not stop me from writing; in fact, it sparked a fire that was dormant inside of me. It forced a girl that I had been hiding to awaken.

Through years of writing and self-inspection, I have discovered that I have a story to tell. My whole life, I never really spoke aloud. I did not think that I really had anything important to say, and, really, I did not think that I had anything to offer. I felt stifled and worthless. I spun in a world of self-hatred and self-harm. One night, like so many, I lay in my bed hiding my tears from my family, scribbling in the dark. I felt broken. I stayed up for hours writing poetry. The next day I decided to read what I had written. Before that day, I never reread the things I wrote in the night hours. Each piece was like a puzzle, revealing more and more truth as I read. This day marked the moment where I realized that I was truly broken and needed help. It was as if another woman was whispering secrets to the pages at night. I read words that bound my identity to pages, sewn with intricate threads. They screamed that I was worthless and that I should sink into the depths and let the water fill my lungs, never to rise again. That day, I vowed that I would never let anyone decide who I was and whether or not I mattered.

Something that rose from my writing was the realization that I had created a god that hated me and that I believed I was created only to suffer. I lived in a world that wanted my voice silenced. I decided that from that day on, I would in turn, silence the very voices that tormented me. Nevermore. I knew that I had to change the way I saw the world, saw God, and saw myself. That day began a journey into my past. I knew that if I didn't face the demons that had a hold on me, I could never break the terror that consumed me—the past I had forgotten.

There is a small girl locked in the back of my mind. She sits by a tree, alone in the front yard. She is broken and I have to find her and tell her that everything is going to be okay. I want to hold her hand and tell her she is loved and that she is worth something. And if there is an audience, perhaps they are others, locked in jars, who need to hear what I have to say.

She

She is encased in a glass jar. Like an antique, dusted moth. I am afraid to let her out. She might crack. She may fall apart in my hands, her memories dusting my fingers. She sits there. So silently, so well trained. Kneeling gracefully under the pepper tree in the front yard, she traces the sandy figure eight over and over. Dandelions brush against her thigh in the breeze. As soon as I see the flies buzz near her sugar crusted eyelashes, I have to look away.

I want to throw the jar.

Summer Preserves

In the back of the yard
behind the swaying Queen Anne's Lace,
jagged cattails catch my stockings.
Bleached by the sun,
crumpling, curled painted boards
shelter the jars
my grandmother boiled in the kitchen last summer— tomatoes, peaches,
  and woodsy blackberries
line the shadowed shelves.
Dusty and dank—
the light creeps in through cracks
sparkling on corners of quilted jam—
blinding, burning in my nostrils
the autumn heat.

Panic

The plates, they spin with graceful ease and golden rims. It all might break.
I hold them all in place—
nothing left of myself. It all might break.
Toss them to me, more than I can hold, I'll find a way. More than I can
    hold. I can't catch my breath—panic. It all might break.
Waves and waves. Spots float—flicker.
Spinning in the air.
The back of my throat dries. My swollen tongue sticks, thick. It all might
    break.
The breaths come quick, too fast. I am dazed—stunned—dilated.
They fall and fall and fall and spin and warp and trip.
It all might break.
He looks at me and questions my ability to spin. I knew I was never
    qualified.
They break into shards.

Fragments

My memories are forever locked in Mason Jars boiled tight.
Years and years and years of lost scents that awaken,
pictures torn in pieces—fragmented, laughter and giggles.
The shed holds them all on broken shelves laced with acrid dust—hiding
   the broken ones spilling and crusting
sticking to each other, mixing together
the crackling walls bend in the angry son's glare.
He sits on high, wondering if I will ever break— splintered, cracked, and
   warped
with all my might holding the jars
with the
memories of a girl I have forgotten.

Stirrings

I sit in the water so deep that I can float my arms above my shoulders and sink my head down so only my nostrils can save me. So hot that my skin feels numb underneath it. I imagine all the stories that could have been. I see white dresses in the cerulean sky. Hot breezes—floating scarves. Dogs barking at hopping birds. I think of the stitches and scars that hold my body together. That hold my memories together. The feeling of sinking and desperately grasping for roots I never had, hoping to crawl back out. Holes that were never filled. Holes that were filled, but I couldn't accept it. I feel deep stirrings of love and regret. Ripping my insides as it pulls. My heart feels like it might collapse inside of itself. I imagine what it must feel like to have my wrists submerged in this water, watching the crimson swirls as I fall asleep. Forever.

Coffee Canned

Words and images, thoughts and moments
are those of poetry
Snapshots of emotion where my grandmother stood
singing country classics, pouring bacon grease in the coffee can and my
  cousin came in to have breakfast again.
We could hear the cows out by the fence this morning.
But if you don't know where to put the comma, don't put one because
then you forced me to stop and pause when I wasn't planning on it
but I want to pause—now,
And running and running and running until I can feel my breath at the
  back of my throat like the words you forgot to say to me last December
when I wanted to write them down in my journal
filled with words and images—
I couldn't find you my whole life and then you sat on my couch for four
months watching Westerns and eating my cornbread that tasted like
your mother's or mine or whatever—
My poetry is jarred like peaches that have waited years in the
cabinet because we forgot about them.
They are sweet but are tainted with old memories and
my grandmother's wedding ring is at the bottom of the jar—I guess
that's where it went.

Poetry should never be told what to wear or where to go
or how to sound.
It should just be poetry.
It should remember my mother's long hair in the wind in Fontana
with the cactus outside the yard
and the neighbor's dog that killed cats in the night
and the rusty Nova that drove through my dreams but couldn't stop
and strawberries on a Saturday sprinkled with sugar
and the demons that crawled out of my heater vent near my yellow room
the tree branches that scraped the glass outside—
and my cousins that disappeared. And my aunt that loved me
even if I was disheveled.

The periods should come when I finish. They should stay if they want.
Poetry should piece me back together.
Poetry should piece us all together.
My voice is here, mangled and sticky under years and years
of inadequacy. Right next to yours.

Felicity

Queen Anne's lace lines the slick black pavement bending in the wind,
   they sway.
Far back in the left corner, behind the corn fields a white house with black
   shutters peeks
through the maples.
Lonely miles curve in and out
of corn and soybeans—beaten, rusty mailboxes.
I rub the wild flowers on my face and close my eyes. My gut twists as
   pangs of memories
tenderly stroke my nostalgic, sentimental
mistaken childhood filled with chicken dumplings and blackberry cobbler—
my drunken father stumbling through
olive oil stained doorways.
Heroin and alcohol seep in the soil here
in Felicity.

Don't Ever Tell Anyone What Happened

The walls are lined with your words they linger like memories that whisper
my name over and over
They crawl in my skin
over and under, through and within stuck in my fingernails
too deep to pull clean
Longing to sing in the winds— The sirens reach out their hands to capture
   the power that flits in and out of your predicate dominated sentences
pulling me under the water
green hands they grab—your words and suffocate my thoughts
longing to silence my
grace
my serenity
my calm
ebbs and tides
envelope me—your words they lull me
even though you are gone— your power lives
through the words
that line my walls.

Speak to Me

Never keep anything unless it speaks to you. Never follow anything unless
    it speaks to you. But
what if it speaks to me and I don't want to hear it hum softly in the night
in the back of the closet that I shut
ten years ago?
That speaks to me.
Voices that I shut
finger locks—
mechanical inconsistencies let them slip.
Never let them speak to you Never let them force you
to
accept
what they whisper. Accept
what they whisper. Except that it is the truth. It speaks to me.

Outer Space

In the dark
I sit here and wonder, wander, ponder
the ledge that sits in the kitchen, above the sink
my thoughts they creep along the ceramic tile my husband chose
there against the wall with the windows, above the ledge, above the sink
   they lurk
and crawl outside the window, just there above the ledge, above the sink
   through the crack.

It Must Be Asthma

My heart beats so incessantly. It is so bothersome sometimes. It comes up in my throat like a child stamping its feet, wanting what he can't have. Pounding on the glass doors with both hands in my chest. I can't hear you, it's so loud. All I can hear is the screaming in my ears. I can't breathe. It must be asthma. Maybe I had too much caffeine. Maybe I need to lay down. Maybe I am broken.

Triage

The spirits speak and I hear
the whisper scrape against the window pane.
Echoes of branches in the wind.

Memories tap, scratching
at the back of my haunted spaces, locked
deep under the fog, floating.

He reaches deep in the aquamarine.
I can see his hand, stretched—
eyes wide with no words.

sleep paralysis—live paralysis
I know He sees me, garbled words,
the glass separates the water from the air

There is no room for us both
to occupy the depths—no
understanding, no air.

Enmity. Between light
and dark. Between Him and me.
Loss of words. Loss
of self.

Anxiety Is my Mistress.

I play at her lashes.
I flirt with her long legs and cumbersome thighs. I long for her to lay hold
    of me.
To take me.
To finally destroy me.

I Woke upon the Curve of Dawn

I woke upon the curve of dawn and listened to the misty sky
the darkness of the moon caressed the edges of the silver clouds
and I wondered why in this empty solitude, I would find myself filled with
    the spirit. The haunting and beautiful voice
of the one who spoke into my soul
alone on the windowsill—
the raven
flew across the yard through the laced black leaves
of my neighbor's ancient maple
and he looked at my face—
nevermore, would I feel empty
nevermore, would I feel lost
because he hears my voice
in the misty morning sky.

Flight

The song goes on and on, she sings
from the accursed branch outside the door Get up, move on, set flight
  with wings.
They stir in the back of my mind, like ghosts. Memories locked tight
  behind smoky walls— The song goes on and on she sings.
Whispers of lost visions, voices I remember— their urgency wakens my
  idled cortex.
Get up, move on, set flight with wings.
Though bloodied from their patina bars— turquoised, rusty stained
  phrases float. The song goes on and on, she sings
I sit, too many keys to unlock—
in the bottom of the abyss, this cage—I can't Get up, move on, set flight
  with wings.
And she, perched high, with silver wings—
her delicate voice, helpless—gasps for air, still... the song goes on and on,
  she sings:
Get up, move on, set flight with wings.

Guardianship

Papers. Hundreds of papers stapled together. These should be filled out in triplicate. You may need a lawyer but you shouldn't *didn't I say this would be hard?* I mean, I thought we would have her but now it's too hard. These papers confound even the strongest man with the most intelligence—he sits there. *i don't even think i have what it takes to change anything i mean life is a cycle isn't it?* These papers these court papers they have power don't they? Can you write me a letter that describes my character? Can you say why she should be mine and not theirs, why it's better for her to admit that her parents love themselves more than they pretend to love her with Barbies and old seventies songs? How they trained her to be a princess locked up in her castle with demons crawling down below? If you sing a song and dance really nice, people will love you. If you take it, they didn't really need it anyway if you are pretty no one will know that she lost her teeth because he pushed her into the coffee table and that he has a hernia because she kicked him hard enough to kill him. No one will know that he has no idea that he doesn't remember what he did to her mother, to my mother, to my aunts and his mother. No one will know that her mother chose that man in prison to give her soul to and that he waits until July to collect. But those papers. They know. It is written in black and white. He has no interest in her. Stapled. In triplicate. my sister's keeper

Mother, Ida Crane—Investigation

Allegation: Neglect, Physical Abuse
She walked in the middle of a road with a stroller
intoxicated, three beers in the stroller
it was raining
Allegation: Child Endangerment
drug abuse
Allegation: General Neglect, Physical Abuse
She couldn't go to school because her father kept them up all night—
with his drinking
Allegation: Child Endangerment, General Neglect
Received phone call, the father needs to pick her up from school because
    mother is drinking It was also reported that the mother is using
    methamphetamine, pills,
and crack cocaine
Alone, she waits at school. Second grade.
I know Allison takes care of Melanie better than I can but I know Melanie
    doesn't really want to be there She lied to me, she told me she would
    bring her
back here to Ohio,
She shouldn't have told me that if she wasn't going to do it. I don't have a
    job,
I am working on that
I don't really have any money
She said the court wouldn't let her bring her here
but I don't believe it
I can't provide for Melanie the way they can
They have all the money and the power
Her daddy wants to fight for her but they have money
I wanna go see her in California If she doesn't want to stay there, she
    shouldn't have to
After I got out of jail,
I got the paperwork where they claimed her dad and I were unfit—We
    used to drink together
I went back to drinking when Allison came and got her

I had a car
My boyfriend Jeff stole it when he got out of prison
I am trying to get sober so I can get my daughter back
I am in a better place now, than I was

        I'm not sober, but I have an interview with Amazon.
                    I just want to see my daughter.

The Woods Are his Home

My father walks alone in the woods
miles and miles line his face
He speaks volumes of lies in his bad-ass stories
of gang members and bar fights
He brought a woman here—
Charlene Butts
We told him to go on his way
as he scoped my yard for a place to hide for the night He cries for Ohio—
for houses he can hide behind
and friendly drug addicts he can rely on
California is dry
and lonely
Even if his daughters are here

Ledge

My daughter shares a room with her ten year old aunt. She sings songs in the dead of night, questioning her importance among the stars. In the bathtub, she cuts herself in places they can't see but leaves the kitchen knife sitting on the ledge. She sulks her way back to the room past the sleeping child who is filled with questions of why she is here and not in Ohio with her own mother and father who have no idea where they are dazed in stupors of alcohol and regret. Which she is she, they don't know because they share the same face and share the same panic in the back of their eyes because this is a normal everyday over and over they don't know why they keep breathing but they do and the girl that is ten watches the woman, 22, and wonders if it is her fate to question the stars and wonders if she too will sit on the ledge of uncertainty like the knife, like her parents. And here I am wondering if this is supposed to be our truth.

My Third Late Night Call This Year

Hey Lola I really needed to talk to somebody tonight. Your mom was tellin' me that after what happened the other night I should get one a those advanced directives. Ya know. I was coughin' for three days. They say all that blood that came up was my sinus cavity. Just came out, all rotted out I guess. The reaper done come for me again I guess. That's the third time I died. Ya remember I tole you I died. They can't kill John Dick. It ain't my time. This time though. This time, I feel 'em followin' me. Ya know. Angie. Angie are ya listenin' ta me. I need that prime directive. Ya know what that is right? If somethin' happens, I'm gonna put your name down. You and Rose. Don't let her unplug me too soon Lola. Ya know I was at the liquor store an this big man walked in and he tole me to give 'em my hat, an I says, "It ain't worth no trouble man," an I give it to'em. Then he tole me to give 'em my cane. So I busted 'em in the mouth with it. I broke his jaw. They asked me if I wanted to press charges. I got my hat back. I ain't pressin' no charges though, ya know. I remember what you said last week about me forgettin' about ye. I was thinkin' about it and I know you think I forgot about you, but I never did. I remember when I was ridin' my bike up Mount Rubidoux with ya when you were little and you got your foot stuck in the spokes, I was yellin' at you, aww hell, I shouldn't have got mad, but I think about stuff like that sometimes. I'm a little high tonight. Ya know. I never heard of nobody coughin' up blood like that with the em- physema, ya know I coulda filled up a coffee cup with how much I coughed up. I sent, you listen to me, I sent your mom checks, the government took it out of my pay. I never forgot about you Ang. Never. I never came around because I was protecting your mother from me. I never forgot. When you left Ohio, I stayed. I sent them checks. Don't let your mom unplug me too soon. I got a little high tonight. I ain't been smokin', I haven't been drinkin' much either. The reaper. He's followin' me. I broke that man's jaw with my cane. You seen it? It's a pretty bitchin cane.

Stone

I walked the way alone for miles and miles. Looking over my shoulder,
  fingers crossed;
at things left behind, memories I lost.
Tired, exhausted steps. Pillow-muffled cries. Stained walls and endless
  windows, woman dies.
All the time I trudged and looked for the cross. All that time I never knew
  I wasn't lost.
Whispers of my grandmother in the sky.
On the porch, he sat, alone in the yard.
I saw the music spin and dance—like God spoke to my chest as it burst
  out like fire.
My fate had been dealt like a Jack on a card. The lonely street we had
  both for years trod— hand in hand we move, never will we tire.
Charity, voluntarily giving good will to humanity generosity, benevolent
  gratitude this institution
Understanding understatements smirking, lurking in windows wishing,
  wanting, longing to hold you afraid to be touched
afraid to touch
terrors of terrors, sweating at night
night sweats in sweaters, you hold me too tight but the light that swings
  and graces your eyes
with the crackle of the fire
stills my panic
and I touch your crackled knuckle,
tracing the outline of the years you worked to keep me whole.

Defense Mechanism

If everything could just stop
And I could sit in the midst of my cloud
This cloud nine that I would rather name eight
The particles floating
So seriously floating and gliding
So close to my lashes
Flitting and diving
Like snow

If everything could just wait
And I could think about how
You made me so angry and lonely and lost
Emotions are raging
My heart is flailing so seriously staging
Feelings on sleeves
Like a show

If everything could just heal
And I could be me in the midst of my crowd
This crowd that keeps battering my self
Pieces keep falling
So desperately falling and falling
As I keep trying to catch them
They are falling
Slipping
My sick show.

Angela LeBlanc was born and raised in Southern California. Her young life was shaped by dysfunction and a constant state of upheaval and nomadic living. She learned very quickly to adapt, finding her place, no matter where she landed. At an early age, this lifestyle helped to shape her view of the world, family, and God.

Never having a true home base in which to find solace, caused a distrust and awkward fear of the outside world. This distrust created a silence of voice for many years. She was not able to adequately express herself verbally and so began a journey by expression through art and writing.

Various traumatic experiences left Angela in a constant state of longing for lost, left, and missing pieces of family. At eight years old, Angela and her mother escaped Riverside heading for refuge in Tennessee. When denied sanctuary, they were forced into the homeless shelters of the city. Eventually, they landed in Ohio with new family. Two years later, she was once again swept away on a Greyhound bus headed for California, hid from everyone she loved. This longing for Ohio still haunts her today and seeps into her writing.

In all of this, there was a constant: faith. Although church had become the center and home base for her, she found herself excluded as she got older. Because of this, her need to find God and the truth that lies in the pages of his word, also lays delicately in the poetry.

Today, Angela lives with her husband, children, and dogs in Riverside, California. She enjoys working with her high school students, reading books, and teaching literature. She finds solace in writing and spending days at the ocean.

www.ingramcontent.com/pod-product-compliance
Lightning Source LLC
LaVergne TN
LVHW021123080426
835510LV00021B/3296